Our Garden

Healthy Living

This is our garden.

We have hens
in our garden.

I feed the hens.

The hens are hungry.

The hens lay eggs.

I get the eggs.

This is our garden.
We have vegetables
in our garden.

11

Look at me.

I water the vegetables.

I pick the vegetables.

I love our garden.